Sher Clain
404-0903

```
D0555096
```

THE CRACKWALKER

Judith Thompson

The Crackwalker

Judith Thompson

Playwrights Canada Press
Toronto • Canada

Playwrights Canada Press
215 Spadina Avenue, Suite 230, Toronto, Ontario CANADA M5T 2C7
416-703-0013
orders@playwrightscanada.com • www.playwrightscanada.com

Playwrights Canada Press acknowledges the support of
the taxpayers of Canada and the province of Ontario through
The Canada Council for the Arts and the Ontario Arts Council.

Front cover painting "Down the Lido" by Helen Healey, photographed by
Steve McKinley. Production Editor: Jodi Armstrong.

National Library of Canada Cataloguing in Publication

Thompson, Judith, 1954-
    The crackwalker / Judith Thompson.

A play.
ISBN 0-88754-621-8

    I. Title.

PS8589.H4883C73 2002   C812'.54   C2001-902335-9

First edition: September 2003.
Printed and bound by AGMV Marquis at Quebec, Canada.

The Crackwalker was first produced by Theatre Passe Muraille, Toronto, in November, 1980, with the following company:

THERESA   JoAnn McIntyre
SANDY   Jane Foster
ALAN   Hardee T. Lineham
JOE   Geza Kovacs
THE MAN   Graham Greene

Directed by Clarke Rogers
Set and costumes designed by Patsy Lang

— • — Characters — • —

THERESA
SANDY
ALAN
JOE
MAN

The Crackwalker

ACT ONE

—•— Scene 1 —•—

THERESA   Shut up, mouth, I not goin back there no more
noway, I'm goin back to Sandy's! *(to audience)* You
know what she done to me? She make me go livin
with her up on Division near Chung Wah's, cause she
say I come from God, eh, then she go lookin in my
room every night see if I got guys in there cause
Bonnie Cain told her I was suckin off queers down
the Lido for five bucks; I wasn't doin it anyways
Bonnie Cain was doin it I was just watchin. So last
night, eh, I'm up there with a friend of mine, Danny,
he a taxi driver – we're just talkin, eh, we weren't
doin nothin, and so she come up and knock on the
door and she say, "Trese I know you got someone in
there" and I go "No Mrs. Beddison ain't nobody in
here," and she start goin on about God and that, and
how she knowed cause she got a six feelin in her, so
I get scared, eh, so I tell Danny to get in the closet.
We don't got no clothes on, eh, so I put his jeans and
that under the bed and I get under the covers like
I'm sleepin and I go "S'kay Mrs. Beddison you could
come in now." So she come in lookin at me like a
stupid bitch and she say she knowed there was
somebody in there cause she heard talkin and I says
"You feelin okay Mrs. Beddison, ain't nobody here
cept me and I sleepin," then she start goin near the
closet, eh, and Danny start laughin. Well she runup
the closet and she pullin on the door and I'm pullin
on her arm and I'm saying "Trust me Mrs. Beddison,
ya gotta trus me," cause the sosha workers are
always goin on about trus and that, eh, but she don't
listen, she open the door and there's Danny standin
stripped naked. Well that whoredog Beddison start
screamin God words at him, eh, so he takes off outa
the house and she takes off after him and I got his
pants, eh, so I throw em out the window case he
catch em and then I bawlin. I bawlin on the bed and
ya know what she make me do? She make me take a

bath! A bubble bath like for the baby! All bubbles and that! Then she make me put on her stupid dressin robe itch my skin and smell like chocolate bars and that and she take me to where she livin and you know what she make me do? She make me read the Bible! I don't like readin no stupid Bible! Ya get a stomach ache doin that, ya do! Stupid hose bag. I'm not goin back there no more no way, I'm goin back to Sandy's.

— • — Scene 2 — • —

SANDY and JOE's apartment. SANDY is scrubbing the floor furiously. THERESA appears, joyous, carrying a plastic bag containing all of her belongings. As she has not seen SANDY in several weeks, she is very excited.

THERESA   Hi Sandy, how ya doin!!

SANDY does not look at THERESA.

SANDY   What are you doin here?

THERESA   I come callin on ya!

In the following sequence, SANDY's anger builds. At first, however, it contains an element of teasing.

SANDY   I don't want no houndogs callin on me. *(continues scrubbing)*

THERESA   I not a houndog!

SANDY   Yes, y'are.

THERESA   No I not.

SANDY   Whoredog houndog that's what you are.

THERESA   *(laughs, delighted)* Sanny!

SANDY	*(pointing backwards)* And get your whorepaws offa my sofa.
THERESA	*(jumps, removes hand, gasps)* Sanny, like I don't mean to bug ya or nothin *(eating donut from bag)* but like I don't get off on livin where I'm livin no more so I come back here sleepin on the couch, okay?
SANDY	I not keepin no cowpies here.
THERESA	I not a cowpie!
SANDY	*(faces her)* Would you get out of my house?
THERESA	Why, what I done?
SANDY	...Ya smell like cookin fat – turns my gut.
THERESA	That only cause I eatin chip from the chipwagon!
SANDY	I don't care what it's cause of, get your whoreface out of here.
THERESA	Why, why you bein ugly for?
SANDY	You tell me and then we'll both know.
THERESA	What.
SANDY	Don't think nobody seen ya neither cause Bonnie Cain seen ya right through the picture window!

THERESA claps a hand to her mouth in "uh-oh."

	On my couch that I paid for with my money.
THERESA	Wha–
SANDY	With my husband!
THERESA	No way, Sanny.
SANDY	*(unable to contain her anger any longer)* You touch my fuckin husband again and I break every bone in your body!

THERESA   Bonnie Cain lyin she lyin to ya she think I took twenty buck off her she tryin to get me back.

SANDY   (*starts speaking after "she lying to ya"*) That's bullshit Therese cause Bonnie Cain don't lie and you know she don't.

THERESA   You don't trus me.

SANDY   Fuckin right.

THERESA   I never done it.

SANDY   Pretty bad combination, Trese, a retarded whore.

THERESA   That's a load of bullshit Sanny, I *not retarded*.

SANDY   Just get out of my house and don't come back. (*pushes her*)

THERESA   No I never I never done it! (*In angry indignation she pushes back.*)

SANDY   Trese Joe told me, he told me what the two of youse done!

THERESA   Oh.

SANDY   Lyin whore, look at ya make me sick. Wearin that ugly dress thinkin it's sexy cause it shows off your fat tits and those shoes are fuckin stupid ya can't even walk in them.

THERESA   I know.

SANDY *stares at THERESA. THERESA does not move.*

SANDY   (*with an air of resignation, tiredness*) Just get out, okay?

THERESA   I never wanted it, Sanny, I never wanted it he come in he made me.

SANDY   Bull Trese.

THERESA   He did I sleepin I sleepin there havin dreams I seen this puppy and he come in and tie me up and push it in me down my hole.

SANDY   What?

THERESA   He tie me all up with strings and that and he singin Ol Macdonel Farm and he say he gonna kill me if I don't shut up so I be quiet and he done it he screw me.

SANDY   Are you shittin me?

THERESA   And – and – and he singin and he take his jean down and it all hard and smellin like pee pee and he go and he put it in my mouth.

SANDY   He could do twenty for that.

THERESA   Don't send him up the river Sanny he didn't mean nothin.

SANDY   Horny bastard he's not gettin into me again.

THERESA   Me neither Sanny he tries anything I just run up to Tim Horton's get a fancy donut.

SANDY   Oh he won't be cheatin on me again.

THERESA   How come Sanny, you tell him off?

SANDY   Fuckin right I did. After Bonnie tole me, I start givin him shit, eh, and he takes the hand to me callin me a hag and sayin how he liked pokin you bettern that and look *(reveals bruise)*

THERESA   Bassard.

SANDY   He's done it before, but he won't do it again.

THERESA   Why, Sanny, you call the cops on him?

SANDY   *Right.*

THERESA   Did ya–

SANDY   Ya know my high heels? The shiny black ones I got
up in Toronto?

THERESA   Yeah, they're sharp.

SANDY   (*obviously enjoying telling the story*) And he knows it,
too. After he beat up on me he takes off drinkin,
comes back about three just shitfaced, eh, and passes
out cold? Well I'm there lookin at him snorin like a
pig and I says to myself "I'm gonna get this bastard,"
I'm thinkin of how when I seen my heels sittin over
in the corner and then I know what I'm gonna do.
So I take one of the heels and go over real quiet to
where he's lyin, and ya know what I do? I take the
heel and I rip the holy shit out of his back with it.

THERESA   JEEZ DID HE WAKE UP?

SANDY   Fuckin right he did. You shoulda seen him, first
I guess he thought he was dreamin, eh, so he just
lies there makin these ugly noises burpin and that?
And then he opens his eyes, and puts his hands up
like a baby eh, and then I seen him see the heel. Well
I take off right out the back door and he's comin
after me fit to kill his eyes is all red he's hissin I am
scared shitless; well he gets ahold of me and I says to
myself "Sandy this is it. This is how you're gonna die.
You got the bastard back and now you're gonna die
for it." Well he is just about to send me to the fuckin
angels when he stops; just like that and turns around
and goes on to bed.

THERESA   How come he done that, Sanny?

SANDY   I didn't know at first either, then I figured it out.
Cuttin him with the heel was the smartest thing
I done. Ya see, he wasn't gonna kill me cause he don't
want to do time, eh, and he knew if he just beat up
on me he'd never get no more sleep cause I'd do it
again. He knows it. He don't dare take a hand to me
again, no way. Either he takes off, or he stays and he
treats me nice.

THERESA   Did you talk to him later?

SANDY   I ain't seen him for three days. But we ate together before he took off, I fixed him up some tuna casserole and we ate it; we didn't say nothin, though. It don't matter, we sometimes go a whole week without talkin, don't mean we're pissed off at each other.

THERESA   Al and I talkin all the time when we go out.

SANDY   We did too when we first started goin together. After a while ya don't have to talk cause you always know what they're gonna say anyways. Makes ya sick sometimes. What are you bawlin for?

THERESA   I'm sorry Joe done that to me, Sanny.

SANDY   He's like that, he's a prick.

THERESA   S'okay if I come livin here then?

SANDY   ...Sure, I don't care.

THERESA   Thank you Sanny.

SANDY   I like the company.

THERESA   Don't say nothin to Al, eh?

SANDY   What if I tell him what Bonnie Cain tole me about you blowin off queers down the Lido?

THERESA   Oh no, Sanny, don't say bout that.

SANDY   I guess old fags in Kingston are pretty hard up.

THERESA   You want a donut, Sanny?

SANDY   No. What kind ya got.

THERESA   Apple fritters.

SANDY   Jeez, Therese, ya ever see how they make them things?

THERESA   No, I never worked up there.

SANDY   It'd make ya sick.

THERESA   I love em.

SANDY   I know ya do, you're a pig.

THERESA   Fuck off.... Only kiddin.

SANDY   You watch your mouth.

THERESA   You love Joe still?

SANDY   I don't know. I used to feel like we was in the fuckin movies. Member that show "Funny Girl" where Barbra Streisand and Omar Sharif are goin together?

THERESA   She hardly sing pretty.

SANDY   Well remember that part where they start singin right on the boat, singin to each other?

THERESA   Yeah.

SANDY   We done that once. We'd been up at the Manor, eh, Chesty Morgan was up there so we'd just been havin a hoot, eh, and Joe wants to go over to the General Wolfe to see the Mayor, so we get on the Wolfe Island ferry and we're laughin and carryin on and that and then we start singin, right on the bow of the Wolfe Island ferry.

THERESA   Jeez.

SANDY   We didn't care when we were doin it though, we didn't give a shit what anyone was thinkin, fuck em we were havin fun.

THERESA   I love singin.

SANDY   Joe really done that to you?

THERESA   What?

SANDY   *Raped* ya.

THERESA   Don't like talkin about it Sanny.

SANDY   *Trese.*

THERESA   He done it when I never wanted it it's true.

SANDY   It is, eh?

THERESA   S'true, Sanny. Don't tell Joe, eh?

SANDY   I mighta known it.

THERESA   Still okay if I sleepin here though?

SANDY   You're gonna have to do the housework while I'm workin for Nikos.

THERESA   How come you workin down there I thought you didn't like Nikos?

SANDY   I get off on corned beef on rye, arsewipe, what d'ya think I need the fuckin money.

THERESA   Ain't Joe drivin for Amey's no more?

SANDY   No.

THERESA   What's he doin?

SANDY   Fuckin the dog, I don't know.

THERESA   Bassard.

SANDY   I know. Gimme a bite of that.

THERESA   I not really retarded am I Sanny?

SANDY   Just a little slow.

THERESA   Not like that guy walkin down street lookin at the sidewalk?

SANDY   Jeez he give me the creeps.

THERESA   He hardly got the long beard, eh?

SANDY   I know.

THERESA   Not like him, eh Sanny?

SANDY   No. No, I tole ya Therese, you're just a little slow.

THERESA   Oh.

> *JOE and ALAN barge in with a hot motorbike. They start quickly, efficiently taking it apart and packing the parts. SANDY and THERESA stand there stupefied.*

JOE   Ya hoo! We got ourselves a shit-hot mother!

ALAN   Did we *ever*!

JOE   Okay nice and easy we don't want to mark this babe.

ALAN   Like this?

JOE   That's right buddy – fuckin back door wide open shit that dog just sittin there waggin its tail at us.

ALAN   He wanted to be buddies with us.

JOE   I just about shit it was fuckin helpin us.

THERESA   What kinda dog was it Al, one of them golden?

JOE   A shepherd.

ALAN   A German shepherd a police dog.

JOE   A fuckin screw dog.

SANDY   You're not bringin Martin over here.

JOE   How's my pussycake doin? Eh? *(kisses SANDY)* Eh pussycake?

SANDY   I says you're not bringin Martin over here.

JOE   Don't worry babe we're meetin him over to the Shamrock he ain't comin here.

ALAN   Down the Beachcomber Room.

THERESA   That's hardly nice down there all them trees and that?

ALAN   You like it there?

THERESA   I love it.

ALAN   I'll take ya there sometime.

SANDY   Where you been the last three nights?

JOE   Paintin the town brown honeysuck whata you been doin?

SANDY   I said where were ya for three nights in a row?

JOE   Out with the Mayor, poochie, spookin out the Royal.

THERESA   You not out with him he dead.

ALAN   Theresa.

THERESA   He is dead.

ALAN   Joe's only kiddin, Trese.

SANDY   You tell me where ya been or you're out on your ear. I said where were ya the last three nights?

JOE   Just hold on to your pants sugar crack first things first. *(madly working on the bike)*

ALAN   This is big bucks ya know.

SANDY You don't have to tell me cause I know. I know where ya were you were down the Embassy pissin our money away.

THERESA Them ugly old Greeks down there anyways.

ALAN You were takin Papa's *shirt*, eh Joe?

SANDY I'll tell ya somethin about gamblers youse do it just so's you could lose it's true that's why.

JOE Well fuck me blind I never knew that. Did you know that Al?

ALAN Nope, I never heard of that.

JOE Thars pretty good commander, where'd ya get that offa?

SANDY It happened to be in the *Reader's Digest*, arsewipe, and it was written by a doctor, Doctor John Grant, and I guess he knows what he's talkin about.

JOE Oooooh *Reader's Digest*, shit-for-brains is going smart on us.

THERESA She not a shit-for-brains you stupid.

JOE You simmer down there burger.

SANDY Is that where ya were, pissin away my money?

JOE *(completes a physical action)* Gotcha.

SANDY Eh?

JOE Hand me the pliers, would ya?

SANDY *(screeching)* I said where were ya Joe!

> *JOE spits his mouthful of beer in her face. ALAN laughs and laughs.*

That's cute.

THERESA   Stupid dummy-face.

                JOE spits on ALAN. ALAN laughs, spits back.

SANDY   You are cut off and I mean it.

JOE   From what, bitch, your ugly box?

                SANDY exits to clean up.

                Don't know what she's so pissed off at nice brew in the face cool ya right down.

THERESA   I'm movin back here Joe Sanny said I could.

ALAN   She did?

JOE   Is that right.

THERESA   Sleepin on the couch that okay Joe?

JOE   Sure, fuck, I don't care, long as the two of youse don't gang up on me.

ALAN   Two women together always do.

THERESA   What do two women do?

ALAN   You know, gang up on the guy.

SANDY   *(entering)* Only if he got it comin to him.

JOE   Do I get it comin to me commander?

SANDY   You're fuckin right you do.

JOE   Little diesel dyke this one see what she done to me?

ALAN   Holy Jeez!

JOE   She's a live one all right Pearl Lasalle the second.

THERESA   She not like Pearl Lasalle Pearl Lasalle ugly lookin.

JOE   She fights like her though don't ya honey suck?
      What's for supper I'm starvin.

SANDY Nothin.

JOE   What?

SANDY You don't bring in money we don't get no supper.

JOE   Well fuck – don't we got stuff for samiches?

SANDY Nope.

JOE   Well fuck I'm goin over to Shirley's.

SANDY When.

JOE   Right now fuck.

SANDY Take your stuff with ya.

JOE   Would ya sit on this first I want fish for supper.

SANDY Pig. I says take your stuff with ya and get out.

JOE   You for real?

SANDY Fuckin right.

JOE   All right I been wantin out of this hole. Thanks
      babe.

SANDY Is that right?

JOE   Take care. *(starts to go)*

SANDY You could get in a lot of trouble rapin a retard Joe.

JOE   Pardon.

SANDY I said you could get in a lot of trouble rapin a retard.

      THERESA is motioning No! No! No! to SANDY.

JOE   Yeah that's right you would. So?

SANDY   You'll be up the river for twenty years when I tell the cops what you done, Joe.

ALAN   Over fifty don't get you twenty years no way no way!

SANDY   I'm not talkin bout the bike.

JOE   What? What are ya talkin about eh?

SANDY   About rapin a retard.

JOE   What?

SANDY   About rapin Theresa.

JOE   What.

SANDY   About rapin Theresa with me in the next room.

JOE   Rape? Rape? Who told you that did Theresa tell you that.

SANDY   Yeahhh.

THERESA   No no Sanny not rape I only said he done it when I never wanted it.

JOE   Did you tell my wife that I raped you Theresa? *(THERESA doesn't answer.)* Did you say that? Eh? *(grabs her)* Eh?

THERESA   I never – leave me alone you big ugly cock–

JOE   I'll tell you somethin about your little girlfriend buddy. I'll tell you something about this little–

ALAN   It don't matter, Joe, it – it – it just don't matter nobody don't believe her anyways.

JOE   This little girl who's callin rape was sittin on that couch beggin for it.

ALAN   She never.

SANDY   Theresa?

JOE   It's true. I come in piss drunk I'm passed out on the floor and there she is down on all fours shovin her big white ass in my face.

THERESA   No I never.

JOE   Big white bootie right in the face.

THERESA   Go away.

JOE   Tell em like it was Trese, and no crossin fingers.

THERESA   I never say that Sanny, I never mean he rape me!

SANDY   Theresa is he tellin the truth?

ALAN   Theresa you never done that, did ya? Shown him your bum?

JOE   This is your last chance, burger, now tell the fuckin truth or I get serious.

SANDY   Don't lie to me Theresa. I can forgive a lot of things but not a lie.

ALAN   You can tell the truth, Theresa, I'll take care of ya.

SANDY   Eh, Trese?

     Pause.

THERESA   *(laughing)* Who farted?

ALAN   I never did.

JOE   Eh Theresa?

ALAN   It's – it's okay, Joe it's – she – she can't handle her booze yet she was probably drunk or sniffin and you was drunk and it don't matter, it just don't matter I'll be stayin with her all the nights from now I'm gonna take care of her it won't happen again she won't never say nothin bout ya again I promise.

THERESA   You stayin with me all nights from now Al?

ALAN   I'm takin care of ya. I'm–

SANDY   Could youse leave us alone, please.

ALAN   Who, me and Theresa?

SANDY   If you don't mind.

ALAN   Sure, sure. We–

THERESA   Wait for me Al I wanna get some chocolate bars and that I starvin... well I am I didn't have no dinner.

JOE   You. You watch your mouth, eh?

SANDY   Would youse just take off?

> *ALAN pulls THERESA out.*

THERESA   See youse later don't do nothin I wouldn't do.

— • — Scene 3 — • —

> *ALAN and THERESA exit. JOE is furious and trying to cool down. His back is to SANDY. She is aware of his anger. She picks something up off the kitchen floor and starts to take it in to the kitchen. JOE grabs her as she tries to pass him and throws her to the floor.*

JOE   You CUNT.

SANDY   Keep away from me–

JOE   I'm a fuckin rapist cause a fuckin retard SAYS so?

SANDY   Touch me again and you go to your goddamn grave!

JOE   FUCK maybe I'm the maniac been carvin all the TELLERS out in SASKATOON! *(makes monster face and noise)*

SANDY   Go jump in a hole.

JOE   *(grabs her, hard)* What is fuckin with your BRAIN, woman?

SANDY   I didn't mean it.

JOE   It was a *joke?*

SANDY   I was just – you said you liked her better.

JOE   What?

SANDY   You said you liked – pokin her better.

JOE   *(laughs, almost hysterically)* So I go to the joint.

SANDY   I wasn't gonna tell nobody–

JOE   You're a fuckin CROW, you know that?

SANDY   I was just – seein–

JOE   *(thrusting her away)* Get away from me.

> SANDY *starts to run toward him, trying to scream but the sound is muffled and distorted by a stomach seizure which stops her about three feet away from JOE.*

You got your upset stomach again?

SANDY   Bastard.

JOE   *(looks her up and down)* You just give me a hard on.

> SANDY *spits on him.*

Hewww you like it when I'm rough with ya, don't ya? Eh? *(moves her roughly, whispers)* Makes your nips stand up when I'm rough with ya.

*SANDY's hands are still raised. SANDY and
JOE are a foot apart throughout the interchange.
SANDY looks at him with hatred.*

What, you don't want it? Okay, see ya later!

He starts to leave.

SANDY   *(head down)* Joe.

JOE   What can I do for ya?

SANDY smiles.

Oh, ya do want it. Okay, why – why – don't ya take
that blouse there off?

She removes her blouse.

Hm. And the skirt.

*She removes her skirt. She is left in a bra and
pantyhose with a low crotch. He nods, looking
her up and down.*

How come ya like it like this? Eh? *(shakes his head)*
I gotta be somewhere.

*JOE exits. SANDY remains onstage, not moving.
Lights out quickly.*

—•— Scene 4 —•—

THERESA and ALAN are in a restaurant.

THERESA   Where d'ya think Joe took off to?

ALAN   I don't know probably drinkin, maybe the Shamrock.

THERESA   You think they're splitting up?

ALAN   I hope not.

THERESA   Me too. I love Sandy, she my best girlfriend.

ALAN   I – Joe – he and me are good buddies, too. They go good together anyways.

THERESA   Could I have a donut?

ALAN   What kind, chocolate? I know you like chocolate.

THERESA   I love it.

ALAN   Sandy's nuts, you're not fat.

THERESA   Don't say nothin about it.

ALAN   You're not.

THERESA   I don't like talkin about it.

ALAN   Here. Two chocolate donuts.

THERESA   Thank you Alan.

ALAN   Jesus you're a good lookin girl. You're the prettiest lookin girl I seen.

THERESA   Don't talk like that.

ALAN   I love screwin with ya. Do you like it with me?

THERESA   I don't know – don't ask me that stuff dummy-face.

ALAN   I like eatin ya out ya know.

THERESA   Shut your mouth people are lookin don't talk like that stupid-face.

ALAN   Nobody's lookin. Jeez you're pretty. Just like a little angel. Huh. Like a – I know. I know. I'm gonna call you my little angel from now on. People gonna see ya and they're gonna go "There's Trese, she's Al's angel!"

THERESA   Who gonna say them things?

ALAN	Anybody.
THERESA	They are?
ALAN	Yup.
THERESA	You're a dummy-face.
ALAN	So beautiful.
THERESA	Stop it Al you make me embarrass.
ALAN	You're – I was always hopin for someone like you – always happy always laughin and that.
THERESA	I cryin sometimes ya know.
ALAN	Yeah but ya cry the same way ya laugh. There's somethin – I don't know – as soon as I seen ya I knew I wanted ya. I wanted to marry ya when I seen ya.
THERESA	When, when did you say that?
ALAN	I never said nothin, I just thought it, all the time.
THERESA	We only been goin together for a little while, you know.
ALAN	Let's get married.
THERESA	Al stop lookin at me like that you embarrassin me.
ALAN	Sorry. Did you hear me?
THERESA	Yeah. Okay.
ALAN	When.
THERESA	Tuesday. I ask my sosha worker to come.
ALAN	No. Just Joe and me and you and Sandy. Just the four of us. I want Joe to be my best man.

THERESA   Sandy could be the flower girl. Uh. Oh.

ALAN   What?

THERESA   Hope you don't want no babies.

ALAN   Why. I do! I do want babies! I get on with babies good!

THERESA   Not sposda have none.

ALAN   How come? Who told you that?

THERESA   The sosha worker, she say I gotta get my tubes tied.

ALAN   What's that?

THERESA   Operation up the hospital. They tie it up down there so ya won't go havin babies.

ALAN   They can't do that to you no way!

THERESA   I know they can't but they're doin it.

ALAN   They don't have no right.

THERESA   Yah they do Al I slow.

ALAN   Slow? I don't think you're slow who told YOU that?

THERESA   I ain't a good mum Al I can't help it.

ALAN   Who said you ain't a good mum?

THERESA   All of them just cause when I took off on Dawn.

ALAN   Who's Dawn?

THERESA   The baby, the other baby.

ALAN   You never had a baby before did ya? Did ya?

THERESA   Las–

ALAN   You didn't have no other man's baby did ya? With
              another guy?

              Pause.

THERESA   No, it's Bernice's.

ALAN   Who's Bernice?

THERESA   My cousin my mum's sister.

ALAN   Well how come you were lookin after her baby?

THERESA   Cause she was sick up in hospital. Jeez Al.

ALAN   Well – what happened whatdja do wrong?

THERESA   Nothin it wasn't my fault just one Friday night
              I was sniffin, eh, so I took off down to the plaza
              and I leave the baby up the room, eh, I thought
              I was comin right back, and I met this guy and he
              buyin me drinks and that then I never knew what
              happened and I woke up and I asked somebody
              where I was and I was in Ottawa!

ALAN   He took you all the way up to Ottawa? That bastard.

THERESA   I never seen him again I thumbed back to Kingston.
              (crying) I come back to the house and the baby's
              gone she ain't there so I bawlin I goin everywhere
              yellin after her and never found nothin then I see
              Bonnie Cain and she told me they took her up the
              Children's Aid she dead. So I go on up the Aid and
              they say she ain't dead she live but they not givin her
              back cause I unfit.

ALAN   Jeez.

THERESA   I ain't no more Al I don't sniff or nothin.

ALAN   Them bastards.

THERESA   Honest.

ALAN   I know. I know ya don't and we're gonna have a baby and nobody ain't gonna stop us. We're gonna have our own little baby between you and me and nobody can't say nothin bout it. You're not goin to no hospital, understand?

THERESA   But Al she say she gonna cut off my pension check if I don't get my tubes tied.

ALAN   Fuck the pension check you're not goin to no hospital.

THERESA   Okay Al.

ALAN   Come here. You're not goin to no hospital.

THERESA   You won't let em do nothin to me, will ya Al?

ALAN   Nope. You're my angel and they ain't gonna touch you.... Hey! I know what ya look like now!

THERESA   What, an angel?

ALAN   That – that madonna lady; you know them pictures they got up in classrooms when you're a kid? Them pictures of the madonna?

THERESA   The Virgin Mary?

ALAN   Yeah. Her.

THERESA   I love her I askin her for stuff.

ALAN   Yuh look just like her. Just like the madonna. Cept the madonna picture got a baby in it.

THERESA   It do?

ALAN   She's holdin it right in her arms. You too, maybe, eh? Eh? Hey! Let's go up to the Good Thief.

THERESA   Al I don't know you goin to church! You goin every Sunday?

ALAN	No I never went since I was five I just want to go now. We'll go and we'll – we'll like have a party lightin candles and that a party for gettin married!
THERESA	I love lightin candles.
ALAN	Maybe the Father's gonna be there. They're always happy when someone's gettin married we could tell him!
THERESA	Al I gettin sleepy.
ALAN	Well after we party I'm gonna put ya right down to sleep over at Joe's. I won't try nothin or nothin.
THERESA	What if Sandy be piss off.
ALAN	No Trese, they said we could stay there together. The two of us. And we're gonna.
THERESA	Okay... really I lookin like that madonna?
ALAN	Just like her. Just like her.

He is rocking her in his arms. Lights fade.

—•— Scene 5 —•—

JOE	Me and the Mayor we'd pick up a couple steak hoagies, and a case of twenty-four, head up to Merton on the hogs – catch some shit group – you know, Mad Dog Fagin, Grapes of Wrath, somethin, get shitfaced then go back to Kingston, pick us up some juicy pie down at Lino's or Horny Tim's, drive it out to middle road, fuck it blind, and have em home by one o'clock. Then we'd go down and catch the last ferry to the island and fuckin ride from one end to the other all fuckin night. Seven o'clock we'd go into Lou's have us some home fries and a couple eggs easy over then head on back to work in Kingston. That was when I was drivin a Cat makin a shitload of money just a shitload. Huh – the Mayor was fuckin crazy wasn't nothin he wouldn't do nothin

he was smart too he went to university in the States even, he just didn't give a shit about it, you know? He had about a hundred books I seen em all filled with words that long *(measures two feet)* he knew what they meant, too, every one of them but he never let on, ya know? He never let on he knew so much... we never *talked* about shit, it was the shit we done together made us good buddies. Just doin stuff with a guy you know you're thinkin the same. Anybody touched him I woulda killed them and same goes for him... he was a damn good driver too but he wasn't drivin, Martin was. Fuckin Martin fuckin stoned on STP. Martin – Martin wasn't an asshole, but he stupid you know? Jeez he was stupid. So this Friday night we'd all gotten pissed up the Manor, eh, then we all went over to the island just to fuck around and to see the Mayor's sister, Linda, who was workin at the General Wolfe waitin on tables. So Bart, that was his real name, Bart and me and Martin had all got these new boots over at the A1 men's store really nice you know, all leather, real solid a hundred bucks a pair so we wanted to show em off to Linda, you know, bug her. So Bart gets in there and he's jumpin on tables, eatin all the limes and cherries and that for the drinks singin some gross song about his love boots, he called them. Fuck it was funny – we were killin ourselves but Linda she wasn't laughin her boss was gettin pissed off so she told Bart, she goes "Bart, get the fuck out of here I think your goddamn boots are shit." That's what she said. So he give her a big kiss right in front of her boss and we take off in Martin's car. Me and the Mayor in the backseat, Martin and his girlfriend in the front. Well we're headin down the road goin south it's dark but it ain't wet and the last thing I remember Bart looks at me and he says "I wonder what it's like to fuck an angel" and bang everything goes fuckin black. When I come to I'm in the fucking ambulance goin across to Kingston and Bart's lyin there beside me dead only I didn't know it and there's his sister Linda right there in the ambulance. I don't know how she got there – she's all red all black under her eyes and that and she's bawlin just bawlin up a storm and she's huggin his legs and she's sayin something only I can't make out

what she's sayin I can't make it out I was so out of it
I'm thinkin I'm gonna die I'm thinkin I'm gonna die
if I don't make out what she's sayin so I kept tryin to
make it out and she kept sayin it and then I knew
what she was sayin and you know what it was? ...She
was sayin she did like his boots. "I do like your boots
Bart I do like your boots Bart I do like your boots
I do like your fuckin boots I do like your boots I do
like your boots I do like your boots...." She wouldn't
fuckin stop it.

— • — Scene 6 — • —

ALAN and THERESA are sound asleep. The
room is sometimes lit by passing cars. Noise of people
on the street. THERESA's steady breathing.
Suddenly we hear JOE, very drunk, half singing.
As soon as ALAN hears him he springs into his
jeans, legs shaking, and awkwardly tries to light
a cigarette. His heart is racing. JOE enters.

ALAN   Hey Joe.

JOE   Jeeeeeeezus you gimme a scare what are you doin
               here?

ALAN   Stayin with Trese member? Member ya said I could?
               The – the mum's got company – in from Windsor.

JOE   Windsor – What a fuckin hole.

ALAN   Yeah it's hot down there – in the summer–

JOE   Look what I found in the fuckin hallway. Cheese
               samich with a bloody Kleenex stuck to it.

               This makes ALAN very sick.

ALAN   Jeezus who put it there.

JOE   I was thinkin maybe the wife left out a little snack
               for me. Ya want some? Blood'n Cheez Whiz samich?
               Hey hey hey it's hardly good.

ALAN	Hey no – no – no thank you. No way.
JOE	What, you don't like eatin blood or somethin?
ALAN	I never tried it.
JOE	Were you screwin that?
ALAN	No! No I mean no I was just I–
JOE	Why the hell not?
ALAN	Oh no I mean I was eh, like I was a couple hours ago, but not right before ya came in I wasn't.
JOE	Jeez you're strange. How come ya got dressed you goin out?
ALAN	No – no I'm not goin out – I – I couldn't fuckin sleep, you know? Ya know what that's like? Ya just keep turnin and can't lie right? So I thought I'd wait up and just shoot the shit with you when ya came in.
JOE	Strange-o.
ALAN	I guess so. Did-dju play tonight?
JOE	Papadapa dies!
ALAN	He – he was cheatin again?
JOE	Fuckin right he was.
ALAN	He dies.
JOE	Greasy fuck. Fuck once I seen Edwards get him in a half Nelson an he was so greasy he slipped out!
ALAN	Ewwww.
JOE	Slipped right out. Slimy bastard right in the middle of the game I turn to him and I says "Papa" I says, "Don't fuck with me, just don't fuck with me."

ALAN	That's hardly good. Huh. What did he say?
JOE	Nothin. He just made one of them noises.
ALAN	What, what the ones with their mouth like this? Like a chicken does?
JOE	Hah. Yeah it is kinda like a chicken. Gives me the creeps.
ALAN	Yeah. Yeah, they do that all the time and the one I worked for, Andy? He *stunk* too, he smelled like matches, you know? After ya light a match?
JOE	He's gettin it.
ALAN	Yeah?? Yeah? Who's gonna give it to him, are you? Are you gonna give it to him Joe? I'll help ya I hate the bastard. I hate him.
JOE	Buddy I am pleadin the Fifth. Fuuuck. *(singing)* "I gotta get outtaaa this place if it's the lassst..."
ALAN	I know what ya mean, Joe. Too – too – too bad there weren't no late movie on or something – hah – Mr. Ed or somethin.
JOE	Who's he when he's at home?
ALAN	Mr. Ed? The talkin horse, don't ya remember? "A horse is a horse of course of course and no one..."
JOE	Hey *(indicating bedroom)* w'she bawlin or did she go out?
ALAN	Sleepin when we come in I think.
JOE	She's a good woman buddy.
ALAN	I know she is Joe. So's Trese.
JOE	Are you sure, buddy?

ALAN   Oh – that was – she – she didn't mean nothin honest Joe she she just don't think sometimes, ya know?

JOE   That mouth of hers is gonna send her up shit creek one day ain't it burger?

ALAN   You – you want a smoke?

JOE   Whaddya got – menthol, fuck, I can't smoke that shit.

ALAN   I know – I didn't buy em a guy a guy give em to me.

JOE   Hey hamburger sorry for wakin ya.

THERESA   I not a hamburger.

JOE   Ooooh I thought ya was!

THERESA   You shut up I sleepin.

JOE   Okay burger queen. Yeah. Yeah buddy she's okay too.

ALAN   Thank you, Joe. So's Sandy.

JOE   She never fucked around on me, you know.

ALAN   No?

JOE   Not once. *(goes to window and leans out)* What a fuckin hole this is eh? ...K fuckin O. *(yells out window)* Fuuuuuuck.

          SANDY enters.

SANDY   Would you shut it?

JOE   *(singing)* "I gotta get out of this place."

SANDY   Why don't ya then ya big pig.

JOE   I told ya woman don't go callin me pig in public. Jeez she got an ugly mouth, eh?

SANDY	You're shitfaced, Joe, go on and pass out.
JOE	You make me wanta piss my pants.
SANDY	Just go on makin a fool of yourself.
JOE	Down woman, me and my pal Al is gonna head up to Horny Tim's and we're gonna pick us up some tailerooonie! Then we're gonna go on over to the quarry and we're gonna get ourselves sucked and fucked–
SANDY	You're not proud, are ya.

JOE bumps into something, falls. SANDY starts to pick him up.

JOE	You never fooled around on me, did ya?
SANDY	Nope. I never... did.
JOE	*(sings)* "She's a hooo-o-o-o-nky tonk womannnn gimme *(goes to bedroom)* gimme gimme the *(fading)* honky tonk wom...

ALAN goes to the window and silently mouths "Fuuuuck," in imitation of JOE. He turns on TV, crouches on sofa, and sings softly, but can't remember the whole song.

ALAN	Nobody – nobody here – but us chickens, nobody here but us guys don't – don't bother me we got work – to do we got stuff to do and eggs to lay – we're busy – chickens– *(He pretends to be a car, makes sounds, mimes a steering wheel.)* Neeowwwwwwwwwwww. Whaaaaaa. Fhrhuuummmm. Atta girl.

—•— Scene 7 —•—

Later, SANDY brings in bedding to sleep on sofa, turns on lamp, turns off TV, lights cigarette, sits on sofa.

SANDY	He pukes all over the fuckin bed.

ALAN   Oooh shit.

SANDY   Funny.

ALAN   I'm – I'm sorry Sandy I didn't mean to laugh at ya.

SANDY   Can I ask you a personal question?

ALAN   Yeah, yeah sure – what?

SANDY   Am I gettin ugly lookin?

ALAN   What?

SANDY   You know, mean lookin, uglier lookin.

ALAN   Shit no, jeez – you – you look nice I think ya do!
               Who, who said that?

SANDY   No one. Are ya sure?

ALAN   Sure, sure I am you're a good looker I even heard
               people say ya was.

SANDY   Who, who said that?

ALAN   Alf. Alf said ya was.

SANDY   His folks are loaded.

ALAN   I know!

SANDY   Did – did Joe ever say anything?

ALAN   Joe? What about?

SANDY   About me gettin ugly, *arsewipe*.

ALAN   No, no Joe never said nothin.

SANDY   Are ya sure?

ALAN   Yeah. Yeah he never – he never said nothin! No!
               Why?

SANDY	None of your business.
ALAN	What's buggin you, you got your pains?
SANDY	No, I don't got my pains but I'm gonna get em if youse – if youse – well – no offence or nothin but when are youse gettin outa here anyways?
ALAN	Soon as I get up the money I – wh – why is – is it buggin you me and Trese sleepin over?
SANDY	Yeah. Yeah, it is it's – it's me and Joe gotta have – have some privacy, ya know? Ya know?
ALAN	Yeah. Yeah I do I – I'll be out soon what can I say, we'll be out as soon as I got the cash.
SANDY	I never heard of screwin your girlfriend on your buddy's floor.
ALAN	I'll be out as soon as I got the cash, okay?
SANDY	It's just strange you goin with Trese on our floor.
ALAN	I know it's strange I know I'm strange I'm strange okay?
SANDY	I know you're fuckin strange all right.
ALAN	You're smokin too much. You're smokin too much.
SANDY	Look who's talkin.
ALAN	Well at least I know I'm doin it you don't even know. *(takes drag off cigarette)*
SANDY	You're fuckin nuts, you know that, nuts.
ALAN	I may be nuts but I fuckin know what I'm doin. I know I'm killin myself smokin these I know it so I'm throwin them away okay? I'm throwin them away!

ALAN rips up his cigarettes and takes SANDY's cigarette out of her mouth.

Fuckin killsticks!

SANDY   *(tries to stop him)* Stop it you – fuckin don't you touch me – you fucker you give me back the cash for those right now right now hear?

ALAN   No! No Sandy I can't I don't have the money I gotta save it so I can fuck off outa this hole I don't have money okay??

SANDY   *(starts to back out the door shaking head)* You're nuts Al–

ALAN   *(grabs her back into the room)* I am not nuts. I am not nuts you understand? I just decided now I'm gonna quit smoking that's all. I got a flash in my head of my old man tryin to take his breath tryin to find the fuckin air and not gettin it fuckin all hunched over so's he wouldn't drown to death his his his feet all puffed all that shit all that shit comin out of his mouth and they wouldn't even clean it cause they said he couldn't get nothin cause he was gonna die so he had all this shit comin out of his mouth and and I know he didn't like it cause he was clean – all the time he was washin – and then when he's dyin they don't give a shit about his goddamn mouth with all the fuck comin out of it and they got a goddamn vacuum cleaner goin – we can't hear nothin and he keeps sort of movin forward movin ahead in his chair like when you're tryin not to crash out at the show so ya keep movin forward? He didn't want to go he didn't want to go at all and he went cause of these. Cause of these goddamn ugly white killsticks these! *(shows her cigarette, lets her go)* See? See why ya can't smoke? See?

SANDY   *(very moved by ALAN's speech; speaks quietly)* I don't know who the fuck you think you are tearin up the place just cause you seen your old man fuckin croak.

ALAN   You don't know what it's like, man, you don't know what it's like till you been there don't you talk.

SANDY   Don't tell me what I know, arsewipe, don't you tell me nothin. I seen my mum go, I sat by her bed for

three fuckin months and I don't go carryin on like a
three-year-old.

ALAN   It wasn't the same I'm tellin ya it couldna been the
same.

SANDY   And I'm a woman and I don't go cryin about it
I never cried about it once.

ALAN   I'm not cryin about it I never cried about it I'm just
tellin ya why not to smoke.

SANDY   You're just tellin me shit. Jeez if Joe seen you just
now he'd think you were some kind of fag.

ALAN   I'm not a fag that's one thing I'm not I'm not a fag.

SANDY   Then start acting like a fuckin man.

ALAN   I'm not a fag you take that back.

SANDY   I'm not takin nothin back for no baby.

ALAN   I said take that back you ugly bitch.

ALAN grabs her. SANDY throws him to the floor.

SANDY   You're sad, you know that? You don't scare nobody.

ALAN   I'm no fag.

SANDY   *(goes back to lie on couch)* I seen ten-year-olds fight
better than you.

ALAN   Why?

SANDY   Why what?

ALAN   Why don't I scare nobody?

SANDY   Cause you're a wimp that's why. Like one of them
dogs that starts shakin when ya go to pat it.

ALAN   How come.

SANDY How am I supposed to know?

ALAN Don't say nothin to Joe, eh?

SANDY What, about takin a fit?

ALAN About you thinkin I'm like one of them dogs.

SANDY I won't.

ALAN Or Trese.

SANDY Don't worry about it.

ALAN You watched your mum go?

SANDY Big deal.

ALAN Couldna been the same.

SANDY It's all the same.

ALAN Don't you feel nothin?

SANDY Well I'm not a baby like you.

ALAN No.

SANDY Anyways, bein dead ain't no different from livin anyway.

ALAN How do you know?

SANDY I just know. It's just like movin to Brockville or Oshawa or somethin. It ain't that different.

ALAN Oh no. Oh no you're wrong I think you're wrong there.

SANDY No I'm not.

ALAN Yes you are.

SANDY You don't know shit Al.

ALAN	I do I do know some things and I know that. I know it's different.
SANDY	Get out of my house.
ALAN	I'm goin I didn't want to stay anyways it smells funny in here.
SANDY	Garbage stinks up a place.
ALAN	And Sandy.
SANDY	*What.*
ALAN	No offence or nothin, but you – you – are – you are gettin ugly lookin.

SANDY looks at him.

See ya.

— • — Scene 8 — • —

JOE, SANDY, ALAN, THERESA sitting in bar. Otis Redding's "I've Been Loving You Too Long" is playing.

JOE	That's a shit-hot tune. Too bad he died.
ALAN	Did he die?
JOE	That's right. In a fuckin motel.
ALAN	That's too bad.
JOE	Too bad Jimi Hendrix died too.
ALAN	Yeah. Oh *yeah. (sings, drums)* "Scuse me while I kiss the sky!"
JOE	Did youse know if Hendrix hadda lived he was gonna join up with ELP?

SANDY	I seen them, Emerson, Lake and Palmer, down in Montreal.
JOE	Ya know what they woulda, been called if Hendrix hadda joined up with them?
ALAN	Hendrix, and...
JOE	*(wits it out)* HELP. Help. And you fuckin would need help hearin those two play together.
ALAN	Fuck would ya ever.
JOE	Fuckin straight.
ALAN	Would ya ever. Fuck, your brain'd die.
JOE	HELP. *Help.*
THERESA	I wouldn't need no help.
SANDY	You don't got no ear for music.
THERESA	I do so.
ALAN	She sings and that all the time.
THERESA	I seen Jerry uptown he got a job workin for Wilmot's.
SANDY	That right eh.
JOE	Splinter what a cocksuck.

> *Restless, JOE goes to the jukebox, presses button. JOE walks to the urinal. After a moment, ALAN follows.*

THERESA	He be workin with all that ice cream all the time.

> *Pause.*

SANDY	He could hardly munch out.

THERESA   I love ice cream.

SANDY   Just munch right out.

— • — Scene 9 — • —

JOE and ALAN. In urinal of bar.

ALAN   Those two guys together. Geez! *(shaking head in disbelief)*

JOE   I'm goin buddy I'm takin off.

ALAN   Where ya goin?

JOE   That's for me to know.

ALAN   Oh. Sorry. How – how come gettin sick of Kingston?

JOE   Got me a job drivin a Cat.

ALAN   Jeez. You make a lot of cash doin that.

JOE   Nice work if you can get it.

ALAN   Nice work if you can get it.

JOE   Make a shitload of money.

ALAN   That's hard to do, drivin one of them things, ain't it?

JOE   They're mother fuckers.

ALAN   Jeez fuck where'd ya learn how to do that anyways?

JOE   Hymie Beach.

ALAN   WOW, I never knew that. You live down there?

JOE   Sure, shared a motel room with this creep who later turned out to be a queer boy. Started sayin stuff about my dink and that when I got out of the shower. "Is it always that long?"

ALAN   Fuckin queers.

JOE   I know.

ALAN   They just make me – feel like pukin–

JOE   I sent that one through the fuckin wall.

ALAN   Did ya?

JOE   Fuckin right.

ALAN   I hate em.

Pause.

JOE   Don't say nothin to Sandy.

ALAN   Don't she know?

JOE shakes his head.

What if something happens – she gets cancer or somethin?

JOE   What?

ALAN   Them things happen, I've heard of them.

JOE   ...I'll let ya know where I am.

ALAN   Hey – I'd like to do that kind of shit.

JOE   You should come out. You could get on a site dry-wallin or somethin.

ALAN   They just take anybody?

JOE   Sure.

ALAN   No, no way.

JOE   Suit yourself.

ALAN	Hey – I forgot to tell ya, Cathy Yachuk jumped offa the Brock Towers!
JOE	What?
ALAN	Jumped right onto her feet Martin was sayin, fucked em up so bad they hadda take a piece of her bum and glue it on to her f-f-feet – so's she could walk on them.
JOE	How come she done that?
ALAN	She seen a white light in front of her, tellin her!
JOE	Fuckin whore... yuh, I'm gettin right out of this hole.
ALAN	You comin back ever?
JOE	How'm I sposda know?

— • — Scene 10 — • —

ALAN on way to work, stumbles out door. There is an Indian MAN on the street, his wrists bleeding heavily. He is ambling past ALAN. He is very drunk.

ALAN	Hey buddy – hey can I do something for ya?
MAN	*(drunk, mumbling)* Please...
ALAN	Hey, want a smoke?
MAN	Yeah. Give me a smoke.
ALAN	What are ya lookin for man?
MAN	Fuckers took it fuckers.
ALAN	Who? Did somebody jump ya? Eh? Did somebody jump ya?
MAN	Yaah. Some guys. Buncha Indians – fuckin Indians.

ALAN	Hey man you're an Indian aren't ya?
MAN	*(giggling)* Don't burn the fish bones! Don't burn the fishbones!
ALAN	That's okay man my fiancee she's Indian. Therese. I like Indians it's okay.
MAN	*(weeping like a girl)* Stupid fuckin Indians.
ALAN	Hey. Hey don't cry. Is it hurtin bad? Please – just stay here – I'll call an ambulance. Stay. *(starts to walk to phone, holds up hand)* Stay.
MAN	*(sits up, screams a death scream)* Aaaahh!

> *ALAN comes back, takes off his own shirt, ties it around the MAN's wrist to stop the bleeding. The MAN sees a vision.*

Devil-baby-eyes-devil-baby-eyes. Please. Please. Mercy. Mercy. Hand. Gimme your hand. Hand. Please.

ALAN	What? You want me to hold your hand? Okay.

> *MAN takes ALAN's hand, starts rubbing it in a sexual way. ALAN doesn't know what to do.*

MAN	*(urgently)* Hey. Hey. Hey.
ALAN	What, what is it, buddy?
MAN	Hey. *(makes intercourse motion with fingers)* Let's tear off a piece. Come on let's tear off a piece. Rip off a piece. Come on.
ALAN	Stupid cocksucker!

> *ALAN flings MAN away, but MAN clings to his leg.*

Get off me you fucker! Get offffffff me! *(He runs.)*

MAN   *(lies on street, giggling)* Pleeeease. (giggles)

             ALAN jumps back to SANDY's living room
             where THERESA is asleep at his feet.

ALAN   *(yells)* Dieeeeeeeeeeee!

— • — Scene 11 — • —

It is the middle of the night.

ALAN   Therese?

THERESA   Yeah?

ALAN   Do you ever start thinkin ugly thoughts before ya go
             to sleep?

THERESA   No, do you?

ALAN   Yeah.

THERESA   Like what?

ALAN   Like fallin down and your teeth hittin the sidewalk.

THERESA   Ewwwww.

ALAN   Sometimes I even think of someone takin out my
             spine, like they do with a shrimp.

THERESA   You crazy stupid-face, go sleepin and think of nice
             stuff.

ALAN   Like what.

THERESA   Donuts and the Wolfe Island ferry and that. Stuff
             like that.

ALAN   Huh. I love ya Trese.

THERESA   Madonna.

ACT TWO

— • — Scene 1 — • —

ALAN　　Did you ever start thinkin somethin, and it's
like ugly...? And ya can't beat it out of your head?
I wouldn't be scared of it if it was sittin in front of
me, I'd beat it to shit – nothin wouldn't stop me –
but I can't beat it cause it's in my head fuck. It's not
like bein crazy, it's just like thinkin one thing over
and over and it kinda makes ya sick. Like when I was
a kid and I used to have these earaches all the time,
you know? And I would keep thinkin it was like a
couple of garter snakes with big ugly teeth all yellow,
like an old guy's teeth and there they were the two
of them suckin and bitin on my eardrum with these
yellow teeth. Makin noises like a cat eatin cat food.
I could even hear the fuckin noises. *(makes the noise)*
Like that. Just made me wanta puke thinkin that –
made the pain worse I'd think of their eyes, too,
that made me sick, black eyes lookin sideways all
the time while they keep suckin and chewin on my
eardrum. Fuck. Do youse know what I mean? No
offense or nothin I don't mean no offense I wish
youse all good luck in your lives. I was just – like
I just wanted to know if any of youse like knew of
a medicine or somethin ya might take for this – they
gotta have somethin cause the one I'm thinkin of
now is even worse it's fuckin bad it's it's somethin
Bonnie Cain told me about this nurse she knows
goin out to Enterprise out to one of the farms out
there these folks were on the dole so she goes up to
see if the kids got colds and that, and the wife, all
small with her teeth all black takes her into the
warsh room and tells her she got somethin wrong
down in her woman's part. And Bonnie said this
nurse lifted up this woman's skirt and you know what
she seen? Like a cauliflower growin out of her thing!
A cauliflower! Fuck! And ya know the worst part
of it? When ya cut it it bleeds! It grows blood and
that! It just happened last summer too, last fuckin
summer in July! ...How'd she go – like how'd she pee?
Fuck I'll be doin the dishes where I'm workin down

the Tropicana there and it's like pictures burning holes in my brain I try all the time to like put other pictures over top of that, nice things that I really get off on, eh, that I really like like – like lambs in a field, you know, with the black on their faces? Like baby sheep? I always liked them whenever I seen one in a field or someplace I always laughed at them so stupid lookin and cute fuck – I never told the other guys they were there case they burn them or something. Anyways I try puttin pictures of these baby sheep over top of the cauliflower and I'll do it and it's okay for a second then the lamb its eyes'll go all funny like slits lookin sideways just like them snakes and then it'll open its mouth and there'll be them long sharp teeth and a bunch of worms inside and the nice little sheep goes all ugly on me and the cauliflower comes back worse than ever like it ate the sheep or somethin.... Maybe if I could just have a car or get back to workin on cars, you know? Or get into Dragmasters, then maybe I'd stop thinkin of these things. I don't know. I'm lookin for somebody who knows, that's why I'm askin youse I don't know. I wish I did. *(pause)* If it was in front of me I'd beat it to shit, you know?

— • — Scene 2 — • —

ALAN and THERESA at home. ALAN comes in after work. THERESA is watching television, laughing.

ALAN   Did ya do it did ya get it done?

THERESA   You got somethin on your mouth Al.

ALAN   *(wipes)* What was it?

THERESA   Look like cream from one of them Joe Louis.

ALAN   What I got on my face don't matter, Trese, I asked ya a question.

THERESA   What?

ALAN Did ya get what I told ya done?

THERESA Readin writin?

ALAN Yes.

THERESA Shhhh baby sleepin Al.

ALAN Did – let's see. Awwwww hey Danny! He's not sleepin! Hey ya little bugger how ya doin – this is your dad this is your dad speakin, ya know me? Hey? He does, he knows me. Don't ya Danny. Hey Danny did your angel mummy do what Daddy asked her to? Eh? Yes? She did? Oh thank you Danny you are the most neatest cutest little baby boy – what's that on his chin?

THERESA From eatin milk.

ALAN Theresa you don't eat milk you drink it.

THERESA I know.

ALAN There. Wipe that ugly milk offa ya. Eh Danny? You are my little bugger and I'm your daddy! Hey! Your mummy gonna show me what she done! Okay Mummy, now show me what ya done.

THERESA I lost it.

ALAN How could you lose it?

THERESA I done it, Al, but I lost it.

ALAN Theresa. Theresa I'm gonna try not to get mad at ya but ya can't keep doin this to me! Every day you're tellin me ya lost your homework!

THERESA Maybe someone take it.

ALAN Theresa don't you understand I am tryin to improve my family.

THERESA *(coyly)* Al.

ALAN   What.

THERESA   *(delighted)* You shoulda seen the pooh I done today it was hardly long!

ALAN   Theresa, married ladies with babies ain't supposed to say things like that!

THERESA   Sorry.

ALAN   Danny could hear ya ya know.

THERESA   I don't think he hear Al I think he deaf.

ALAN   What?

THERESA   I shoutin in his ear he don't do nothin.

ALAN   Trese ya don't go shoutin in babies' ears!

              THERESA kisses ALAN. He melts.

THERESA   I love ya Al.

ALAN   You know I love you don't ya you know it – more than anything in this whole world you and Danny boy.

THERESA   I know Al. How many dishes you done today?

ALAN   Two hundred and twenty-three.

THERESA   Jeez.

ALAN   Yup. That's ten more than yesterday.

THERESA   Jeez.

—•— Scene 3 —•—

              THERESA has been sleeping over at SANDY's because SANDY is scared. Cat scream.

SANDY   What's that noise. Trese wake up. Hear that?

THERESA   What?

SANDY   Listen – oh Jesus what is it?

THERESA   Maybe it Charlie Manson.

SANDY   Oh shut up you watch too much TV.

THERESA   Maybe it a pussy cat.

SANDY   Hello? Hello? Anybody there? Trese hand me somethin. The lamp.

THERESA   Why?

SANDY   Shut your mouth and don't ask questions.

THERESA   Okay okay here.

SANDY   Okay. You get the knife from the top drawer just in case he comes in here.

THERESA   Who Charlie Manson.

SANDY   Don't say that name Trese. Scream if anybody comes...

THERESA   I will Sanny.

> *SANDY goes to other room. She screams a primal scream.*

SANDY   *(returns)* It was nothin.

THERESA   How come.

SANDY   Cause.

THERESA   How come my baby never smilin?

SANDY   Are ya doin what the workers tell ya?

THERESA   Al do it he don't let me do nothin.

SANDY	Why?
THERESA	He smarter.
SANDY	I guess so.
THERESA	He love Danny. He wash him with soap and he feed him and he huggin him.
SANDY	What's he feedin him.
THERESA	Bologna.
SANDY	At four months?
THERESA	He love it.
SANDY	Oh Christ. Don't ya have baby food.
THERESA	I don't know.
SANDY	What am I gonna do with you?
THERESA	I'm glad I stayin here. Al cryin nights.
SANDY	How come?
THERESA	I don't know. I tell him nothin's wrong everything fine but he keep cryin.
SANDY	Trese do ya think Joe'll come back?
THERESA	He proly comin back next Friday.
SANDY	If he do, he can go to hell.
THERESA	Bonnie Cain say he never comin back.
SANDY	She did?
THERESA	She don't know nothin. He comin back.
SANDY	I got a letter.

THERESA   Ya did?

SANDY   I burnt it though, didn't read it.

THERESA   Sandy you depress?

SANDY   No. I just don't like stayin alone nights it ain't good for ya.

THERESA   You could come stayin with us.

SANDY   Uh uh. No way. I don't want to see no baby eatin bologna.

THERESA   Oh.

SANDY   You get in some baby food, Trese, or I'm reporting ya to the social worker.

THERESA   Okay.

SANDY   Okay?

THERESA   I'm gonna.

SANDY   You go on to sleep. Now.

THERESA   Night Sandy. Don't go havin no bad dreams.

SANDY   Night.

> *THERESA falls asleep instantly. SANDY stays awake, staring out.*

— • — Scene 4 — • —

> *ALAN has just been fired from his dishwashing job. He is thrown out of a door, real or imaginary, onto a busy street. He has stolen an egg, which he carries in his hand.*

ALAN   *(holding up egg as pointer)* I was quittin anyways, ya bastards, there's white worms in the hamburg, I seen em, there's white worms in the hamburg! *(more quietly, to himself)* I seen em wiggle– *(turning to audience, in threatening tones)* There wasn't no egg on that pan, sir, there wasn't no egg on that frypan.

> *ALAN stares at the audience for a moment, gets the idea to throw the egg at the door and turns very slowly towards door. Then in a flash, starts to throw the egg but instead, cracks it over his head. He puts the shell in his pocket, sees somebody in the distance, sticks down his hair, leans onto the sewer and discovers the Indian MAN with a bottle. ALAN grabs it and takes a sip.*

MAN Man, who is standing between two girly-girls in the whirly-burl.

ALAN Oh why don't ya just shut up...

MAN *(pointing at constellation in the sky)* Double devil – stuck together – cha cha cha!

> *JOE appears, wearing a new coat and a hat that says "SUCCESS." ALAN rushes to greet him. By the end of the scene, they reach the entrance to SANDY's apartment.*

ALAN Jesus Joe! Joe! Hey Joe, how're ya doin?

JOE Hey buddy how are you?

ALAN Okay, you know, hangin on. You – when did ya get back?

JOE Just now, buddy, but not for long. I'm moving Sandy out there with me.

ALAN No kidding? It's pretty good out there?

JOE It's a great place, man, lots of work, nice people. Hell of a lot better than this hole, I'm tellin you.

ALAN Yeah? Does Sandy know you're back?

JOE   Nope. I'm gonna surprise her. She'll be happy as hell to see me. Then the two of us are gonna take right off.

ALAN   That right? ...Hey me and Theresa got a kid – a little boy, Danny.

JOE   Is that right? Danny, huh? So how do you like bein a father?

ALAN   It's all right, man. I like it. I make a good father I guess.

JOE   Yeah? ...Well, I better head off.

ALAN   Hey – Joe – I got somethin to tell ya.

JOE   Is this a long story or a short one?

ALAN   Not too long – d'ju hear about Boyd's GTO?

JOE   What the one that used to be parked on Johnson below Division?

ALAN   Yeah, you know, green with chrome mags and chrome cut-outs.

JOE   Yeah. What a fuckin beast. What about it?

ALAN   He totalled it.

JOE   Hah. Well it was a shitty lookin car anyways.

ALAN   Yeah but fuck it had – it had them high lift cam solid lifters, and, and high compression kit and–

JOE   You name it.

ALAN   He had it. Yup. Hey – did you know it had four fuckin carbs?

JOE   Eat shit.

ALAN   No kiddin, four! But you know how come he kept it lookin so shitty?

JOE   Beats me.

ALAN   So the cops wouldn't notice. They all knew, though eh, they knew what he had. Fuck that thing was fast he used to shoot the main drag doin one-fifty.

JOE   Yeah? That's fast.

ALAN   Fuckin fast. You know how he totalled it?

JOE   No.

ALAN   Fuck it was funny. We were gettin polluted up at the Manor, eh, and Alfie decides he's gonna go up to Gan. He was about half pissed I guess. So parently he tries to pass three or four cars same time except one of em happens to be a truck goin left. So I guess he almost makes it but the truck catches him by his back right fender and spins him. Huh. Flipped the car six fuckin times.

JOE   Jeez. How is he?

ALAN   Alfie? He's okay now but he got stabbed in the heart with the rearview mirror. Had an operation.

JOE   That right?

ALAN   Chuck was with him and–

JOE   The Scotty?

ALAN   Yeah and he just jumped out and never even had a scratch on him. What's that a present for the wife?

JOE   Yeah. That Charlie perfume shit.

ALAN   Hardly nice. Yeah, that's nice stuff. Women – they like that kinda stuff.

JOE   I know. Smells shitty to me.

ALAN	Yeah.
JOE	Well I gotta move buddy catch you later.
ALAN	Hey! Hey!

From his pocket, ALAN takes an ornamental iron monk with a hard on. It is wrapped in newspaper.

	Here.
JOE	What's this?
ALAN	Just somethin.
JOE	Oh yeah. I seen one of these. Well I'm gone.
ALAN	See ya.... Bye Joe!

—•— Scene 5 —•—

SANDY and JOE seated at a table.

SANDY	I got a fucking hole in my gut cause of you.
JOE	Who told ya that.
SANDY	Doctor Scott.
JOE	He don't know what he's talking about.
SANDY	Hurtin me all the time I had pain.
JOE	Not no more. Not no more ya won't.
SANDY	I was takin pills even – prescription!
JOE	I told ya babe I feel bad.
SANDY	I never done nothin to you why??
JOE	Ewwww Christ I missed your body there was times I wanted ya so bad I could taste ya. I'd lie in bed

there and think about you and what ya looked like
stripped naked, think about your nice titties.

SANDY   Two old bags.

JOE   *Nothin* them are peaches.

SANDY   Bullshit. I'm not goin back with ya.

JOE   Yes you are.

SANDY   Can't push me around no more.

JOE   Come on just try it a couple weeks if ya don't like it
you can fuck off.

SANDY   Won't be nothin different.

JOE   It's gotta be different.

SANDY   It'll be the same as before, beatin up on me.

JOE   No way.

SANDY   How the fuck do I know?

JOE   Cause it's fuckin true that's how.

SANDY   I hate you. I hated you all the time you was gone.

JOE   I know.

SANDY   I woulda laughed if you hadda died.

JOE   I never did.

SANDY   I know.

JOE   So.

              Pause.

SANDY   How come ya want me back.

JOE	Don't know. It's dog shit when you're gone.
SANDY	Then why'd ya stay so long.
JOE	Shit Sandy.
SANDY	I was up nights shakin.
JOE	Scared of the crackwalker were ya?
SANDY	He never hurt nobody.
JOE	I missed makin it with ya. Did ya miss it with me?
SANDY	I didn't have no one.
JOE	That's cause you're mine.
SANDY	Is that right.
JOE	*(opens her gift)* Here. Smell that.
SANDY	Hmmn.
JOE	You told me you like that shit.
SANDY	It's okay.
JOE	Soooo. You been workin for Nikos?
SANDY	Some.
JOE	What else you been doin?
SANDY	Learned how to make a new drink.
JOE	What, rum and Coke?
SANDY	That's not new.
JOE	What, dough brain.
SANDY	A Dirty Mother, asshole.

JOE	A dirty mother asshole, what's that?
SANDY	A Dirty Mother! It's tequila, crème de cacao, and milk. It's hardly good.
JOE	Sounds like a chocky milkshake from Mexico.
SANDY	Arsewipe. I got a batch made up in the fridge, you want one?
JOE	Yeah, okay. I'll try one. Gimme a beer with it though.
SANDY	*(goes to the kitchen; from kitchen)* You should give Al a call he's in a bad way.
JOE	Yeah I seen him he looked like shit.
SANDY	They got a kid, Danny.
JOE	He was tellin me.
SANDY	It's a medical retard.
JOE	Fuuuuck.
SANDY	It don't ever move its face – like a doll.
JOE	See this thing he give me?
SANDY	What is it?
JOE	I don't know. An iron monk with a hard on?
SANDY	Jeez where'd he get that, up at Van's?
JOE	I guess so. *(SANDY brings in tray.)* Well fuckin jumpqueen, eh, where'd ya get them glasses?
SANDY	My girlfriend Gail she scoffed em offa the 401 Inn.
JOE	Fuckin eh.
SANDY	They'd cost ya, ya know.

JOE	Hmmm. That's, ahhh that's a shit hot drink.
SANDY	Me and Gail drink it all the time when we go out.
JOE	It's not bad.
SANDY	We always order it only none of em knows how to make it so we have to tell them.
JOE	Yeah?
SANDY	I can make any kind of drink now she taught me.
JOE	What're you doin two women goin drinkin alone together.
SANDY	Who said we were alone?
JOE	Come here.
SANDY	Joe it ain't like that no more.
JOE	Who said it ain't.
SANDY	I did. Keep your paws offa me.
JOE	Jeez you're lookin good.
SANDY	I'm doin my eyeliner different.
JOE	Yeah?
SANDY	Makes my eyes look bigger.
JOE	Nice.
SANDY	I know.

— • — Scene 6 — • —

*ALAN and THERESA's place. THERESA is
playing with the baby. There are tea things set out.
The baby does not respond to anything.*

THERESA Beebeebeebee.... How come you not drinkin your tea, beebee? You got a bad cold? Poor beebee. *(singing)* My little baby is my baby my little Danny is my angel baby I take care of him, and he don't cry or nothin and he ain't never gonna have the crib death neither– *(speaking)* No way Danny, cause I love ya. Al loves ya too but he a bastard sometime I know he don't talk nice in front of you sometime – don't you go goin into one of them deep sleeps beebee – no – hey! Hey baby Danny! Wake up cause that's how them other babies got the crib death! From sleepin too deep! S'true! You darlin little baby! You mine! That sosha worker's hardly nice, eh? Look! *(dangles Joe Louis wrapper in front of Danny)* Look at that baby, you like that? Eh? It's hardly pretty! You come on, come on, gimme a smile beebee; you thinkin too much just like Al that why you so serious all the time. ohhhhh baby *(She rocks him.)* so soff. Skin hardly soff. Hey! I, look like that madonna lady and she holdin baby Jesus just like I holdin you so you mus look like Jesus! Baby Jesus! Oooohhh Danny you my beebee Jesus and I the Madonna lady and Al maybe he Joseph, he make stuff outa wood. You like a little horsey made outa wood carry you down Princess Street when we go to the S & R? I love ya beebee. That a little smile? Oh! Oh baby baby Jesus I love Ya!

ALAN *(comes blasting through the door, starts tearing up the place – medicines, creams, clothes, everything)* No fuckin social worker's gonna fuckin tell me how to run my fuckin life! I don't take this fuckin shit from nobody! Nobody don't tell me what to do and nobody don't tell me how to take care of my baby never! That means you too you fuckin woman – I'm not takin any shit from you neither! There. We're not using any of their cocksucking medicine – they'll try to kill you with it!

THERESA Al! Al stop it!

ALAN They did they killed my dad with all their fuckin medicine! He didn't have no hair and he didn't have no flesh just bones all over and ugly and yellow. No

way Therese no way you could stop me I'm throwin
it all fuckin out! Out the window, watch! There! It's
out the window! Danny! Hey Danny my boy my own
son see? You don't have to be takin any of that ugly
tastin shit no more!

THERESA   But he gonna get numona if he don't take his
           medicine doctor say so! Nurse say he hafta take it
           three time a day or he gettin worse! Doctor sees you
           done that he won't give us no more medicine for
           Danny! You bassard! You bassard! *(She hits him.)*

ALAN   Arsewipe! Don't you know nothin? Don't you
           know them doctors make money offa sick babies?
           That's why they like to keep em sick with all them
           medicines! So they make more fuckin money!

THERESA   I don't believe ya. Doctors are nice they wouldn't go
           makin babies sick!

ALAN   Jeez you're a dumbrain sometimes, Therese, they
           don't give a fuck about our fuckin baby so long as
           they get their TV's and golf clubs and that. They care
           dick! That's why they give em this poison so the
           baby stay sick!

THERESA   It not poison, it good for ya, the nurse say so! She
           don't even have no TV, she tole me. So you're crazy
           I know that stuff good for Danny he gettin better
           already!

ALAN   That baby ain't gettin no better you stupid woman
           you know it ain't. It looks strange. It don't look right
           and that's cause they're givin it all them fuckin
           medicines! Fuck them! So no more!

THERESA   Really would them doctors do that? Really?

ALAN   Fuckin right they would. Bastards.

THERESA   Bastards. How come? How come they hurtin my
           little baby?

ALAN   Money. Money and bucks. Cocksuckers.

THERESA   Well what we gonna do about all his snifflin and
              that?

ALAN   Well I know what to do the social worker even said
              I did. He said I was a great father and you even
              heard him. I was a great father.

THERESA   S'true Alan.

ALAN   Well, it got a cold, right? So if ya got a cold, ya gotta
              get warm, what else? It's fuckin simple and them
              doctors always do everything to make it harder!
              Fuck! So all we do, is ahh – turn on the oven! It's
              easy! Here. Put it to about five hundred – there –
              and open the door like that – and – now bring him
              over–

THERESA   Why? What you gonna do?

ALAN   Just bring the baby over, Trese. Do what I tell ya!

THERESA   Al you not cooking the baby, are ya? *(weeping with
              confusion)*

ALAN   *(laughs)* Huh. Wait'll I tell Joe that he'll laugh.
              Cookin the baby. Right. Jesus arsehole it's just like
              at the farm back in Picton when mum used to sit by
              the stove with Ronny to warm him up that's all! It's
              easy! If a guy's got a cold, warm him up!

THERESA   Oh. Don't make it too hot though.

ALAN   Keep out of it, woman. *(places crib as close to stove as he
              can get it)* There. There ya go Danny! How you doin
              anyway you little bugger – that's right it's your daddy
              he come to make you better! Getcha away from all
              them fuckin doctors! That's right.

THERESA   Al he's coughin! Cant we get back some of that
              cough syrup?

ALAN   Listen stupid we're not usin any of that stuff I told
              ya! Didn't ya hear me or what? Listen. If he's coughin
              we'll just get that Vicks vapour rub that my old man
              used to use.

THERESA That stuff smell too much!

ALAN If it's good enough for my old man it's good enough for my baby Therese. He used to put it all over his chest and his cough be gone the next day. Here.

He puts a whole jar of Vicks over the baby's body.

THERESA Al you puttin too much!

ALAN Don't tell me what to do! Shut up! I know what I'm doin I told ya the social worker said I was a great father! So shut up!

He holds the baby up. It is glistening with the stuff.

There. You're gonna be just fine now baby.

THERESA Al you sure it ain't too much?

ALAN Shhhhh. He's goin to sleep. Come here. I got somethin for ya.

THERESA You did? What'dja get donuts?

ALAN *(opens perfume – orange, cheap, and it has broken in the package)* Shit. It broke on me. It's okay though here I'll put it in a glass. *(He does so.)* There. *(hands it to her)*

THERESA Smell that. That's hardly beautiful Al. Thank you I love perfume.

ALAN I know ya do. Ya like it?

THERESA I love it. It hardly smells nice.

ALAN *(caresses her)* Guess why I brung it?

THERESA Why?

ALAN I love you and you're my angel madonna.

THERESA A-l-l-l-l-l.

ALAN   It's true. Come here angel. Hey. Eh hey. You know
I love makin love to ya. I love fuckin you and chewin
ya out. *(whispers)* I do.

THERESA   I know.

> *ALAN starts to undress her. They start necking
> on the floor next to the baby. THERESA stops
> suddenly.*

Oh oh.

ALAN   What?

THERESA   We can't do it Al.

ALAN   Don't matter if you're bleedin.

THERESA   No I can't do it till I get my new IUD in. Or I get
pregnant again doctor say so!

ALAN   Fuck the goddamn doctors! Goddamn doctors trying
to run my life saying I can't make love to my own
woman to my own wife fuck em fuck em. I don't
care if you get pregnant we're gonna do it when we
want and no doctor's gonna tell us nothin.

THERESA   No! No Alan, please! Get off me you bastard we're
not doin it today no way! No! Get offa me or I callin
the cops.

ALAN   *(He hits her, sends her across the room.)* You stupid dumb
cunt Indian bitch face fat fat retarded whore. I don't
want ya anyways! *(He collapses on floor, now meeker,
almost whiny.)* Alls I wanted was a little lovin anyways
there's nothin wrong with that? A man is sposda get
lovin from his woman ain't he? That is how come ya
get married, ain't it? All I wanted was a little lovin
that's all... that's alllll.

> *The baby is crying.*

Look what you done woman you makin the baby cry!
You stupid bitch!

THERESA gets up to go to the baby.

No! No you stay down I'm the only one who can make him stop cryin. Watch. Hey baby. Hey baby here's your daddy. He's a great daddy, huh? Eh?

The baby is screaming.

THERESA   Take it away from the stove Alan! Take it away from the stove!

ALAN   *(to THERESA)* Shhhhh. *(to baby)* Come on baby stop that cryin Daddy don't like it when you cryin! Shhhh. Now shhhhhh. Gonna buy you a car when you get older – what kind you want, a Monte Carlo? Okay. I'm gonna get you a Monte Carlo. You wait, I'm gonna get work in a station and I'm gonna buy my own and I'm gonna get you anything you want. Okay? Now shhhhhhhh. Stop cryin I'm gonna get you a Monte Carlo didn't ya hear me? Didn't ya? Shhhhhh. Be quiet your mum is tryin to sleep, okay? Shhhhhh! Come on, come on. My little Danny boy baby. Come onnnn. Shhhhhhhh!

On the last "shhh" he squeezes the baby's neck till it dies.

Shhhhhh.

From now on he is very wooden, like a sleepwalker. Looks at THERESA, who is watching in wonder.

It's okay. It's okay it's not cryin any more. See. It's quiet now. It's not cryin. I – I – I done it, see? See? I'm a good father he – you know how come he stopped? Cause I told him he was gonna get a Monte Carlo.

THERESA   What's that?

ALAN   It's a kind of car. It's a place too. One of them south sea islands. Maybe we'll go there, eh? Anyways I gotta go I gotta meet somebody... see ya.

ALAN goes. THERESA looks after him.

— • — Scene 7 — • —

*JOE and SANDY's. ALAN, JOE and SANDY
are watching a Leafs hockey game on television.
ALAN is sitting away from JOE and SANDY,
and he is smoking and loudly eating barbecue chips.
JOE and SANDY are very much involved with
each other and the game, and they virtually ignore
ALAN.*

JOE   Go go go you fucker – Bunnyfuck what are you
fuckin doin – *get him off Nykoluk get him off the ice fuck.*

ALAN   Imlach dies.

JOE does not respond.

IMLACH DIES!!

JOE   Oh LAROUQUE – come on Sittler put that mother
in come on come on FUCK OFF PERRAULT, do it
Daryl hey Martin Martin put it in put it ALL
RIGHT! *(jumps up)* ALL FUCKING RIGHT!

*ALAN jumps up with JOE, leans into the TV, his
face only one inch away from the screen, screams,
wagging his head.*

ALAN   ALLLLL FUCKIN RIGHT!

Looks back at JOE with a little laugh.

SANDY   *(jocularly)* Take a bird why don't ya?

ALAN continues yelling into TV.

JOE   Hey Al don't scare the TV away he–

*THERESA appears in the doorway with a bag in
her hand. She is reminiscent of Cassandra in* The
Trojan Women.

THERESA   YOU TOLE HIM YOU GIVE HIM A MONTE CARLO AND YA DON'T EVEN DRIVE ONE. YA DON'T EVEN DRIVE ONE.

> *Her presence is so strong that she immediately captures their attention.*

I not goin screwin with ya no more Al, no way. No way! You stoppem breathin. I tell him "Breathin baby, breathin" and he not cause *you stoppenim.*

ALAN   *(looking away from THERESA)* She's lyin you guys, stop your lyin.

THERESA   You goin up the river to Penetang Al, you goin there tomorrow and you never comin out for what you done you not goin back with me I goin with Ron Harton he better than you he not stoppem breathin, he still livin up on Division up at Shuter's? I callin him up and I goin steady with him he better lookin you funny lookin I screwin him.

ALAN   YOU lyin fat COW you don't know what you're fuckin talkin about crazy fucking whore-bag – LIAR!

> *ALAN knocks THERESA to the floor, hesitates, grabs two glasses half-full of Dirty Mother, and runs off. JOE follows.*

THERESA   You got a donut, Sanny, gimme a donut.

SANDY   What have ya got in the bag Trese.

THERESA   Ivy, Ivy gimme the bag, I not givin it.

SANDY   What's in it, though.

THERESA   I takin him up the graveyard.

SANDY   What for.

THERESA   I puttin him with Grandma down St. Mary's Sanny, see ya later.

SANDY *(stepping in front of THERESA's exit)* Wait a minute what–

THERESA Fuck off Sanny.

SANDY What's inside it.

> *THERESA giggles. SANDY touches the bag, flinches.*

I'm callin the cops.

THERESA Agghhhhh. You fuckin call anyone I takin one of my fits.

SANDY I'm shakin in my shoes, Trese. *(begins to dial)*

THERESA *(grabs SANDY, rips phone from wall)* You not callin–

SANDY *(gets up, begins to exit, turns around, points at THERESA)* You're not here when I get back and I'm tellin Ron Harton what ya done down the Lido, ya hear me?

> *THERESA stares at SANDY in horror.*

I will, too.

THERESA Okay.

SANDY I mean it. *(exits)*

THERESA *(to baby in bag)* It okay, Danny, don't you be cryin now, you with baby Jesus sittin on the cloud and the Virgin lookin like me she with ya she sittin there wearin that long blue dress goin down to her feet hardly pretty, eh? ...Danny? You still live? You breathin if I breathin into ya? S'okay I'm your mum! *(tries to breathe into baby)* Danny? You dead, eh? You not live. You never comin back, eh. *(puts bag to side, picks up severed phone, does not dial)* Hi Janus won't be doin readin writin today. Somethin happen. Just somethin. The baby die. The baby die. Up at Sanny's. Okay okay I waitin... Ron Harton still livin up at Shuter's? *(hangs up the phone, and picks it up immediately)*

C'I speak to Ron please? Hi Ron, its Trese. S'okay if we start goin together I love ya. Okay, see ya Tuesday.

SANDY enters, breathless, leans against the door. She cannot look at THERESA.

SANDY   Don't want you tellin no stories to the cops, you hear me? Want you to tell em the truth exactly like it happened, okay?

THERESA   Don't like ya no more, Sanny.

SANDY   S'too bad.

THERESA   You a dirty faggot.

SANDY   Right.

THERESA   Not my friend no more!

SANDY   Okay...

THERESA   I not talkin to YOU.

She turns her back to SANDY. She is crying. SANDY notices.

SANDY   You should come out to Calgary sometime – visit.

THERESA   No Sanny, I workin!

SANDY   What?

THERESA   *(tells story joyously with no trace of grief)* Down at Kresge's up with Ivy. Hah! She hardly funny she hardly get pissed off when I eatin icin she yellin "Trese, if you eat one more chocolate icin I tellin Charlie" so I go "You tellin Charlie I tellin on you, Ivy, snitchin butter tarts!" They're hardly good, though, them tarts. Ivy English.... Sorry I can't comin with ya out west, Sanny... Ivy be piss off.

—•— Scene 8 —•—

ALAN and Indian MAN on warm air vent.
ALAN is leaning against wall. He is clanging two
glasses together. This produces a spooky sound.

ALAN   *(pointing to MAN)* You fuckin touch me and I'll break your head.

MAN   Hee hee hee Church'n Mondee all dee Mondee hee hee hee!

ALAN   I will break your fuckin head in!

MAN   *(starts happily, becomes angry as he remembers incident with a paramedic who denied him phenobarbital)* Breakin my fa fa pheno phenobarbidoll – barbidoll – NIGGER, YOU NIGGER!

ALAN   Shut it you fuck, just shut it.

    MAN in panic, rushes toward the audience.

MAN   SHUT THE WINDOW, SHUT THE WINDOW, SHUT THE WINDOW... *(laughs)*

ALAN   Nothing's funny, okay, so – just – STOP LAUGHIN. Just pass out will ya, can't ya just pass out? *(MAN vomits on ALAN's sock.)* Ahhhh fuck you goddamn shit. SHIT! Eccchh you keep your puke to yourself you old fuck! *(crouches, rocking)* I could drive a Monte Carlo I know I could. *(rubbing glasses together)*

    JOE enters, looking for ALAN, spots him, then crosses to him.

JOE   Al?

ALAN   Joe!

JOE   Look – ah–

ALAN   She's lyin Joe, I could drive a Monte Carlo.

JOE	Al?
ALAN	I could drive one easy.
JOE	You could drive any car on the road. Now why don't you come on–
ALAN	I – I – I can't.
JOE	Why not?
ALAN	I – I – I'm too cold, you know? I'm freezin.
JOE	You're okay, ya probably got a flu, ya got a bug, okay?
ALAN	No, no, I don't got a bug I'm just cold, he puked on me.
JOE	So he puked on ya Martin used to puke on ya all the time. Come on – come on out of that shit pit and I'll get ya a coffee.
ALAN	NO. No, I don't want to, I just don't want to, okay?
JOE	Suit yourself. *(turns his back on ALAN, starts to leave)*
ALAN	I done what I done and I done it and I fucked it up so I'm payin for it, get it? I'm payin for it.
JOE	I don't know what ya done.
ALAN	Sorry, Joe.

JOE looks at him, can't think of what to say.

	Joe.
JOE	Yeah.
ALAN	Could ya do one thing?
JOE	What.
ALAN	Tell her I could drive a Monte Carlo. Easy.

JOE I will.

ALAN Bye Joe. *(crouches in previous position, zipping and unzipping his jacket)* "Nobody here – but us chickens – nobody here but us guys – don't bother me we got work to do and eggs to lay – and guys to see–"

MAN SHHHHHHHHHHHHHhhhhhhhhh. *(with no motion, just the sound)*

— • — Scene 9 — • —

SANDY I think it's better off dead. I'm not kiddin ya I'm serious. It don't hurt babies to be dead they go straight on up to heaven no hell no purgatory no nothin no problems. Cause their souls are still white as snow – they ain't had the time to get them black and ugly. Not like the rest of us – oh no if a baby dies he's just fine he don't even know he's dead. Youse shoulda seen him lyin there in that casket he looked fine. They had them little pajamas on him Trese got up at the S and R, the ones with all them dogs chasin cats all over, all yellow? They hardly looked sweet. And they had a big wreath of flowers around his neck so's to hide the strangle – you know the kind you put on your door at Christmas? Like that. It was kinda nice. We all lined up to take a look at him too – first time he got so much attention in his life – nobody broke up or nothin not even Trese. In fact I was scared she was gonna break up laughin. I'm not kiddin ya it don't bug her at all the kid's gone. Jeez y'know I don't know what goes on inside that girl but it ain't what's goin on inside the rest of us. She only got one thing on her mind now that's goin after Ron Harton. Don't ask me why, he looks like the fucking wrath of God. He's a pig too. I don't blame Trese though, I still feel for her even –fuck – this old bag sittin behind me was goin on about how come Trese never went to the hairdressers, you know what her hair is like, eh, right in the middle of the service, so I turn around and I says, "You're gonna hardly think of goin to the hairdressers when your own baby's just been killed by your own husband, ya fuckin old hag." I called her that too, right to her face. Oh yeah I'll stand up for a friend, anytime. I'll tell ya who else I stood up for at that service... Al, and he done it. Oh yeah, I still consider him a friend. No matter what he done, nobody can say what happened in that room; so I walk into the funeral parlour, and I take one of them cookies they got lyin out, you know, just tea biscuits, and I turn around and who's standin behind me lookin me right in the eye but that goddamn Bonnie Cain. She comes up close her breath just reekin and she says to me how she seen the whole thing from the window and how he done it with a plastic bag one of them Glad bags and how Trese was lookin on and laughin. That goddamn holy bitch. "You lie" I says to her and I grab her by the tit and I says "You fuckin hound dog one more word outa you and I send you to your goddamn grave...." He never done it with a plastic bag he done it with his hands. I woulda I woulda broke every bone in her fuckin body and she knowed it too. She didn't say nothin more. Jeez I'll be glad to get outa this hole I'm tellin ya. I won't miss it neither I won't even dream about it. I won't. I worry about Trese but she'll be okay, you know? She'll – she'll go back down the Lido, start blowin off old queers again for five bucks. It's still open it won't never close.... They had them flowers round Danny's neck so's to hide the strangle but I seen it. The flowers never hid it they just made ya look harder, ya know? They just made ya look harder.

— • — Scene 10 — • —

Small struggle off stage. THERESA runs on stage.

THERESA   Stupid old bassard don't go foolin with me you don't even know who I look like even. You don't even know who I lookin like.

The end.

photo by Steve McKinley

Judith Thompson was born in 1954 in Montreal. She graduated from Queen's University in 1976 and graduated from the acting programme of The National Theatre School in 1979. Although she worked briefly as a professional actor, she became more interested in writing. At the age of 25, a workshop of her first script, *The Crackwalker*, was produced by Theatre Passe Muraille. Her work has enjoyed great success internationally. She is professor of Drama at the University of Guelph and currently lives with her husband and five children in the west Annex area of Toronto.